SMALL BUSINESS CYBERSECURITY PLANNING

An Owner's Step-by-Step Guide
to Reducing Your Online Risk

Robert Ruder

IDIC Designs, LLC

ISBN-13: 978-1-7355433-2-1
ISBN-10: 1735543321

Cover design by: Robert Ruder
Printed in the United States of America

DISCLAIMER

Cybersecurity is a large topic. There can be cybersecurity specialists, but no-one can ever claim perfection. Still, cybersecurity must be front and center in every business conversation and in the day-to-day habits of owners, staff, and customers.

This book is not the final word on cybersecurity. My purpose is to move you off the sidelines as a spectator. Only active participants in our digital life can make it more secure for everyone.

Consider cybersecurity as your continuous improvement program.

Every day you create habits around the digital devices and information you handle. Your awareness and knowledge about good cyber hygiene should grow every day. This is the only way to protect the investment you've made in your business while respecting the need of your customers and vendors to be protected as well.

Consider this book to be your 101-level course in the art
and science of cybersecurity.

ACKNOWLEDGEMENT

This book would not exist if it were not for the relationship that I have had over the last 7 years with the Washington Small Business Development Center (SBDC).

The Washington SBDC is part of a national network of more than 1,000 SBDC centers across the country where entrepreneurs and business owners can go for no-cost business consulting and no-cost or low-cost training to help them start, grow or buy/sell a business. The U.S Small Business Administration (SBA) administers the SBDC program and provides about half the program's funding, with the other half coming from state or local stakeholders.

I have had the privilege to work with the Washington SBDC as a consultant to help advance their mission to benefit the thousands of small business owners in the State of Washington who work every day to build a dream worth living.

The topic of this book was a direct result of participating as a subject matter expert (SME) on a Washington SBDC initiative to improve the cybersecurity posture of small businesses in the state of Washington.

If you are not aware of this important program, I encourage you to go to this website to find out if there is more help out there for you that can lead to your business success:

https://www.sba.gov/local-assistance/resource-partners/small-business-development-centers-sbdc

CONTENTS

Title Page

Copyright

Disclaimer

Acknowledgement

Introduction

Part I   1

Risk Assessment   3

Create Your Assets Inventory   14

The CMMC Framework   25

Compliance 101   30

Part II   35

Guide to Part II   36

Physical Protections (PE)   38

Identification & Authentication (IA)   44

Access Control (AC)   51

Systems & Communication Protection (SC)   59

System & Information Integrity (SI)   63

Media Protection (MP)   68

Part III   71

Cybersecurity Policy Template   72

[Organization] Media Protection Policy   73

A Cybersecurity Audit Guide   76

Conclusion   81

About The Author   85

Resources   87

INTRODUCTION

What's at stake is the survival of your business. Your dream of being a business owner did not start with the vision of you going out of business. No one plans to close the shop and walk away.

Yet, every year business owners are forced to do just that because of a cybersecurity incident. The costs incurred with restoring operations, replacing hardware and data, and notifying affected customers and partners are high. The risk that one bad moment can send a small business owner into bankruptcy is high.

The natural temptation is to diminish the thought that such a cyber incident could happen. Owners mistakenly believe that they have nothing of value. Or that their chosen safeguards are adequate.

The fallacy in that thinking is the idea that cyberattacks are based on the value of the target. The truth is that most attacks begin as random hunts for systems connected to the Internet with exploitable vulnerabilities.

Cybercrime is an opportunist's game. First comes the exploit of a vulnerability and then comes the decision about how best to monetize the asset. Today's threats are random, low cost efforts to ensnare as many unwary consumers as possible.

Cybercrime is a mass media business. 'Everyone' is a target.

Once an attacker has a foothold, they take their time to understand who you are, who you are connected to, and what level of access you have.

There are multiple ways your digital assets can be exploited. The attacker wants to make the best possible use of your resources.

Whether it's an employee's computer or the employer/business owner's, the attacker doesn't care. Nor do they care what the name on the sign says.

They are only interested in what private information and assets they can extract or control. Their motivation? The profit realized by selling the data or the access to your computers on the dark web.

Your business is always at risk. And you are likely more responsive to the attacker's demands because your livelihood is on the line.

A fortune 100 company has dedicated staff, massive cyber insurance policies, and hardened technology to fight with. You have none of that, so you are more likely to give in to the attacker's demand.

> *How much is it worth to get your business back online?*

Here are small business cybersecurity statistics put together by Nerdwallet for 2021:

- 43% of cyber-attacks target small business

- 47% of small businesses report a lack of understanding of how to protect themselves against attacks
- 3 out of 4 small businesses don't have the personnel to address IT Security
- The median small business receives 94% of detected malware by email
- 54% of small businesses don't have a plan in place to react to cyber attacks
- Small businesses spend an average of $955,429 to restore normal business after a successful attack
- 91% of small businesses don't have cyber liability insurance.

Small Business Cybersecurity Planning is your first step in keeping your business from becoming one of these statistics.

Inside the pages of this book, you will be introduced to the Cyber Maturity Model Level 1 (CMMC) compliance practices. These practices are becoming the de facto standard for any business that wants to do any business with the Federal or state government.

In 2023, CMMC compliance will become a contractual obligation for these businesses and any subcontractors/ partners that they engage.

One benefit of the CMMC is an emphasis on a growth model that adapts well to small businesses. You don't have to create huge investments upfront. There is no expensive independent audit to qualify.

By purchasing this book, you have made the most important investment in securing your future as a business owner.

Now, all we have to do is help you write your cybersecurity policy...

That's coming up in Part II. But first we're going to cover some preliminary topics.

PART I

RISK ASSESSMENT

As a business owner, you must always assess the various risks that your business faces. Traditionally, those risks have been physical ones like natural disasters, rational ones like making the right investments in resources, and social ones like having the right target market or not hiring someone who would be a bad employee.

Large risks, like that of war, are usually far from our minds.

The Internet has changed all of that.

As our businesses become more dependent on the global network, we have opened ourselves up to risks that we cannot see. Those risks are not necessarily targeted at us, but as steppingstones to others, we become collateral damage.

Yet, the damage is real. The loss of your digital devices, the loss of your reputation, or the stigma of having put your customers at greater risk in their lives can overwhelm any business.

Michelle experienced that.

She was the outside sales rep for my client a few years ago. She showed up for work one Monday morning thinking that this was just another work week. She got her coffee, read her email, and started to think about what Google searches she would run to find her next batch of prospects.

That morning, she decided that she would prospect churches in the local community to see if she could place her product in a prominent place among their weekly social events at the church.

Google supplied her with a long list of churches. Dutifully, she started to click through the results to look for information that she could use.

We never discovered which site was the culprit. Somewhere among the pages, she visited, however, dark magic was at work. She clicked a link. The page loaded and suddenly everything started to change.

A large dark page with white lettering and a lot of red text splashed across her screen...

HACKED! Your computer has been hacked and your files have been encrypted!

Michelle, and by extension my client, was the victim of a ransomware attack. I learned of the attack about 5 minutes before I started teaching a college classroom of students.

My contact called me; it was an odd time for a call from him, so I answered immediately.

John told me something strange was going on that was affecting multiple people. He described what he was seeing on his own computer screen.

"John," I responded, "shut all the computers in the building down. All of them. I have to teach my class, but I will be there as soon as I get out."

When I arrived about 2 hours later, I confirmed the bad news. A ransomware virus had gotten loose in the business.

It attacked Michelle's computer first, but it also reached the file server, managing to encrypt many shared files that affected others. Some of those users attempting to open those files allowed the virus to infect their computers as well.

Our quick response contained the attack; however, it still took us 4 days to clean up the machines and bring all the systems back online.

That is 4 days when the business had to run all of its operations on paper and by hand.

Would your business survive?

As a business owner—or leader—you must always assess the risk you face against all threats to your business operations. Proactive leaders look for signs in mistakes, errors, and current events as warnings that something worse could be just around the corner.

Conducting regular risk assessment and remediation planning is one productive step you can take to ensure that your business is prepared for the unexpected. We cannot control the events, but we can mount a planned and robust response.

Risk Response

Living is a matter of practicing risk management. No action that any of us takes is entirely risk-free. What is important is how the decisions we make impacts the risks versus our desired outcome.

There are only four actions that we can take when facing risk:

Avoidance

Avoidance is the choice to walk away. If you know that some action has a 60% failure rate and that the result of failure would be worse than doing nothing, then you would certainly choose to do nothing.

Would you not?

That's the thing about avoidance. Change is always costly. Sometimes we are willing to pay that cost for the improved results that change can bring.

However, sometimes we know that the loss is not worth the value we gain. For that reason, we just simply choose to walk away.

Acceptance

When we choose to accept the risk, we are throwing our hat in the ring. We know that we could get hurt.

We might not achieve the result we want. But the chance of a negative outcome is acceptable. The cost of doing nothing is intolerable.

Mitigation

Sometimes the risk associated with change can be offset in such a way that the downside of failure can be reversed or eased into something that is acceptable.

These mitigation techniques change the decision criteria because we no longer must consider loss as part of the equation of change. This risk reversal might help us decide to move forward.

However, the mitigation also comes with a price tag. To choose to mitigate, there must be a sufficient gap between what happens if nothing is done versus what happens with the mitigating processes in place.

Transference

A fourth and final way to address risk is to find someone else who is willing to accept the risk (for a fee) and promise to make us whole again if we should experience negative outcomes.

This is what the insurance industry is based on.

Underwriters understand in minute detail what the risk factors of any action are, and they can quantify the costs of negative outcomes. For a fee, they are willing to accept that risk. They are gambling that the negative result will not happen, and you will remain whole.

Every business owner that engages in electronic commerce must understand that there is cyber risk just as anyone who drives understands that there are risks involved with being a driver. The question we need to address is whether the costs of failure outweigh the cost of doing the right thing.

That decision will come down to our assessment of probability and impact.

The Threat Matrix

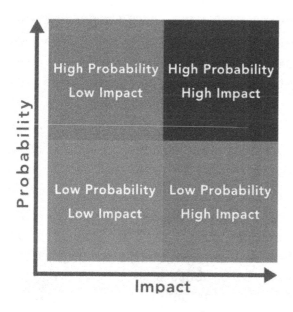

There are two issues that you first address when doing a threat assessment. These are the dimensions that will help us determine where to put our effort in building a response plan:

The first issue is **Probability**. *How likely is it that the event we are imagining will happen?*

Those things that are more likely to happen should be prioritized over those things that rarely happen. This should be obvious to you at this moment.

Planning your meals for the day has a higher priority over

planning what you will say when you are abducted by space aliens.

However, sometimes we get distracted by the novel or scary things that are truly rare. In doing so, we diminish the priority of things that are more likely to occur and have an unknown negative impact on our business.

And that brings us to the next issue: **Impact**. *How much damage can be done to our business because of this event happening?*

When a patient is brought into an Emergency Room with significant trauma, the ER staff are trained in an assessment process that is based on the impact that the trauma has had on the patient's ability to thrive. That assessment follows a simple acronym:

A is for Airway,

B is for Breathing,

C is for Circulation, and

D is for Disability

(*Alert, Voice, Pain, or Unresponsive*).

These simple but vital issues are handled before any treatment can begin on the patient for the issues that brought them to the ER.

In your business, similar issues must be addressed:

- Your business has an airway that allows you to serve your customers—obstructions must be removed.
- You need to address your capability to breath on your own to keep serving those customers.
- Then, you need to look at the circulation which is the means for your business to continue serving customers while experiencing trauma.
- And finally, you need to assess what parts of your business are currently disabled and what affect that has overall on your ability to thrive as a business.

When an incident occurs, your ability to respond will be determined by whether you have created a contingency plan that addresses the situation and whether you triage the effect that the incident has had on the most important systems in your business.

Survivability

Whether your business survives a cyber incident will be directly determined by the amount of effort you have put into the survival planning and training for your business.

There are no right answers to any of these issues. You can't borrow someone else's survival plan.

The critical thing you can do for your business right now is to begin observing your operations like an outside consultant.

Ask HOW questions to uncover the steps and procedures.

Ask WHY questions to discover hidden stakeholders and tribal knowledge.

Ask WHAT questions to discover the systems in place that need protection.

Most importantly, document all your discoveries and then put those documents back in front of your organization. Confirm that you have accurately captured the reality of how your business operates.

Once you have your procedural documentation, then you can look for the areas where you have vulnerabilities that can be exploited.

If you take your results and place them into the threat matrix you can create a prioritized list. This is your gap report which will tell you what your priorities should be.

Next, apply your self to implementing safeguards that mitigate or transfer your risks. Document your processes and create schedules to repeat your tasks to maintain your security practices.

Finally, revisit your list weekly to determine if the business is making progress towards better resiliency. This is your continuous improvement program that will be the key to your survival in business.

Before you can begin your risk assessment, though, you must know what you are working to protect. This is where every cybersecurity plan begins: Your Assets.

We'll take on that task next.

CREATE YOUR ASSETS INVENTORY

I n cybersecurity, an asset is any object—physical, digital, or intellectual—that must be protected. Your assets are what make your business.

Creating an inventory of your assets is the best way to start the cyber planning process.

Not only does it give you raw material, but it reminds you of what your cybersecurity is protecting. Most cyber risks come from hardware, software, or procedures that you didn't know about or forgot.

Make your inventory as complete as possible, giving yourself time to explore the details—don't rush. All the while ask yourself, *"What else do I do with my people, technology, or capital (intellectual and real)?"*

You will know when you have enough material to get started. There is no set word count or an exhaustive list you must achieve. Just capture enough material that you feel informed about the way technology fits in your day-to-day life.

However, remember that Cybersecurity is a continuous improvement project. When you create your inventory, do it in a tool or format that allows you to edit and expand on it. You will return to this list routinely for updates and additions.

The Five Component Framework

You will find a downloadable spreadsheet here that complements this section to help you create your first inventory.
[Resources Page]

To build the right inventory list you need a framework. For our purposes, I propose that the **5 Component Framework of Information Systems** makes a great organizing outline for your need.

The five components we will be working with are:

- Hardware
- Software
- Data
- Procedures
- People

Let's break these down to understand what they are and what you should record about each.

Hardware

Your hardware is any physical device that handles

information you need to protect. Here are some of the things you should be considering:

- Servers (dedicated computers that do work for others, i.e. email, shared database, security, storing files, etc)
- Workstations (computers that stay in one place)
- Laptops (computers that *can* travel)
- Tablets
- Mobile devices/Phones
- Printers/Scanners
- Communication Devices (VOIP, etc)
- Network Devices (Routers, Switches, WiFi Access Points, etc)
- Security Devices (Cameras, Locks—mechanical and digital, etc)
- Data Collection Devices (CNC, Digital monitors, Fitbits, Scales, etc)

You need information about your hardware that will identify it to others. Saying that the files are on the server can be vague. Saying the file is on the *Public* share in the *Contracts* folder on *BusinessFileServer1* is more specific.

When responding to a Cybersecurity incident, more information is always best.

Collect this information about your digital hardware devices:

- DeviceName or Alias
- Device Type: Server, Workstation, Laptop, Tablet, Mobile, etc.
- Device Network ID (also called MAC address)
- Device IP Address (if networked)
- Device Serial Number (good for business

insurance claims, etc)
- Device Purpose/Use
- Device location (physical description)
- Device Operating System (where appropriate)
- RAM Size (running memory)
- Storage Capacity (drive storage)

Another aspect of the hardware is the environment where these digital devices exist. Having physical control over a device is a big concern.

When a threat actor has physical control, there is unlimited time to break down any security procedures that have been implemented.

Collect information about the physical layout of your work environments. Include organizational information that will help you identify where more sensitive information is maintained and managed.

For example, where in your business environment is financial data maintained or handled? Identify those types of places in your procedures and physical location to consider what additional protocols are needed to ensure that the data stays in those locations.

Having maps of your buildings and marking security boundaries such as between public and private areas, etc. is important. Getting information out of one's head and onto a shareable medium like paper or data files is always key to creating effective security.

Consider these ideas when planning your physical environment inventory:
- Buildings where business is conducted

- Physical areas within buildings where public and non-public access is important
- Physical boundaries where security enforcement can be implemented (doors, locks, walls).

As an example, I work with a client who holds very sensitive information that requires above-normal security practices. Since his office is accessed by several other people and the information is housed on a removable storage device, the client has a safe in his office.

When I arrive to work on the project, he opens the safe and provides me with the device so I can do the work that I need to do.

When we're done, the device goes back into the safe. Additionally, all of this access is logged in a logbook.

There are many solutions to any security situation. Your solution will be unique to you. What is important is that you document to show that you took steps to be concerned for the security of your business.

Software

Your software is any form of coding that utilizes hardware to perform a specific task.

Examples of software include Word Processing, Spreadsheets, Email, Web Browsers, Accounting, Customer Relationship Management (CRM), Supply chain management, Social Media, etc.

Don't limit your ideas about what software is important to you. Anything you run to complete a business-related task needs to be included in your Software inventory. But you should also be aware of all the software that others have added—such as the computer manufacturer that adds "free" software when you buy a new computer.

The security concern for software is understanding who produced the code and is therefore responsible for fixing vulnerabilities that expose our systems to hackers.

It is important to know when, where, and how vendors release security patches as well as the best way to apply those patches promptly.

I have a notorious habit of not paying attention to the software on my iPad. A month or more can easily pass while I blithely go through my days without checking to see if the software on my tablet needs to be updated. By the time I do look, I can easily have 20-30 separate applications that need to be updated.

Once again, things that are out of sight are often out-of-mind. Building a routine around maintaining your software is critical to improving your cybersecurity posture.

Here is what you should know about each piece of software you use:

- Name
- Software Type: Operating System, Native Application (designed for your device), SaaS Application (software-as-a-service, cloud)
- Vendor
- Source of Updates
- Purpose or business use of software
- Current Version

Data

Data is the core of your business enterprise. You are in business because of the information that you know that your customers want to know. The value of that information is what they pay for.

This is even true if you are a retail business that handles commodities. If you are a convenience store that carries Snickers bars, it is still the fact that you have a way to buy Snickers bars wholesale so that you can mark them up to retail that matters. Your information matters, so protect it.

What kinds of data do you handle and what are the security implications of that?

Types of Business Data:

- **Supply Chain**: Data about your vendors and raw materials
- **Employee Data**: Data about your employees that may include personal data
- **Customer Data**: Data about your customers that may include personal data
- **Intellectual Property**: Data about unique processes or products that are trade secrets
- **Financial Data**: Data regarding your finances and financial accounts
- **Online Accounts**: Data about accounts you maintain for other purposes related to the business.

These are the details that you record about these types of information that you maintain for your business:

- Business Data Type
- Source of Data
- Authorized Users
- Backup Location

- Access requirements
- Data handling procedures

Your answers here will be more paragraph-like. You are capturing ideas here and not specific data examples. Your procedures will dictate details, but the value of what you work with will be better if you tell your data story.

Procedures

Procedures are the way that you do things. How you do something can have profound security implications. Most people who are always suffering from bad luck or unfortunate accidents are often simply experiencing the consequences of not having a planned procedure to follow that leads to a successful outcome.

Think of Uncle Billy from *It's a Wonderful Life*. It is Uncle Billy who creates the whole crisis for George Bailey because he did not follow a step-by-step procedure to make sure that the money and the deposit slip stayed together.

Having defined procedures that protect your business is the key to your eventual success.

Warning: This is where you can get distracted in building your first Cybersecurity Plan. Remember, the perfect should not become the enemy of the good start. **Cybersecurity is a continuous improvement project.** *What you create today should be reviewed every quarter, refined with new insights, and expanded upon to improve your security posture.*

Start with the divisions of labor in your business—your departments. Within each department outline at least 2-5 separate procedures that handle sensitive data that you need to protect. Document how the procedure interacts with data, software, and hardware.

When you need to reference people who interact with the procedures, define them as Avatars that stand in the place of actual people you interact with. So, labels like HR Manager, HR Data Entry, Accountant, etc are reasonable terms that can be used to understand how something is to be done.

For procedures, you need to consider the following information:

- Business Department
- Procedure Alias
- Actors
- Procedure Objective
- Input Data
- Output Data
- Step Sequence
- Internal/External (who controls the data—you or an external actor)

People

When considering the people—both inside and outside of your business- you need to first think of them as roles or avatars and then as the real individuals who play those roles within your business. Over time people in a role will change, but the demands or needs of the role will stay consistent.

So, for example, the name of the bookkeeper will change over time, but the security and data needs of the person who is filling the bookkeeper role will stay consistent. You, therefore, need to see your business from both points of view.

Let's start with the Avatars:

- Avatar/Role Name
- Answers To
- Needs Access To (types of business data)
- Data Generated
- Required Rights

The key to roles is to think in general enough terms that you don't limit the future needs of a person in that role. However, don't be so vague that you also expose too many people to information that could be damaging if it were leaked or exploited.

Now, let's consider the individuals in your business:

- First Name
- Last Name
- Role/Avatar
- Date of Hire
- Date of Termination (for historical tracking)
- Account Identifier (username/other)
- Account Creation
- Account Termination

A person in your business may wear many hats—like yourself for instance. So, once you have your avatars and your data needs, you next create a grid that maps the avatar to the types of data required to be successful and the level of access and controls the role needs over that data.

With the grid completed you can now look at the people currently acting in the various roles in your business and verify that they have the appropriate access—and no more —that they need.

Summary

Completing an inventory of your environment can be tedious. But not doing an inventory can be devastating. Cyber incidents and breaches occur when you are not focusing your attention. Most cybersecurity incidents happen in the weak links or the unexplored corners of the digital environment.

This step is your due diligence.

If you work with a Managed Service Provider (MSP), they will likely have tools that can speed up this process by scanning your network for all known or invisible devices. These lists can be great starting places for building your inventory.

If you work from home or in a shared office space, remember that your inventory list may be larger than you imagine. One of the notorious cybersecurity attacks ever conducted was notable because many of the devices used were "nanny cams" purchased by concerned parents. A flaw in the operating system allowed attackers to take over control of the cameras to use them as weapons. You don't want to be a statistic.

Nothing takes the place of physically reviewing everything you can find about your network, devices, data, procedures, and people. Your cybersecurity audit could be the first step in a complete business analysis that will lead to improvements in everything you do.

THE CMMC FRAMEWORK

I n the technology world, well-known practices protect you from cyberattacks. Those practices are based on the study of previous attacks against others. When we build our security plan, we must learn from the mistakes and successes of those before us.

Therefore, we call the practice of implementing our cybersecurity response based on established practices **compliance**.

We don't make up rules. We don't try to guess what our vulnerabilities will be. Instead, we follow a set standard of practices that have been tested and retested as generally agreed upon best practices.

In this book, our compliance standard will be the **Cyber Maturity Model (CMM) Level 1**. In the United States, the Department of Defense (DoD) and the Department of Homeland Security (DHS) require all businesses contracting with the Federal Government to comply with some level of the CMMC based on the sensitivity of the data that they manage as part of their government contracts.

Advantages of the CMMC

The CMMC framework is a continuous improvement model. Instead of creating an exhaustive list of practices that every business must meet, the CMM certification levels recognize that businesses change over time. The business cybersecurity practices must mature as the business grows.

The practices that the CMMC requires are based on stable and well-recognized National Institute of Standards and Technology (NIST) cybersecurity recommendations. The NIST 800-171 recommendation, for instance, involves more than 110 separate cybersecurity practices. But the CMMC certifications break those requirements down into levels of compliance that encourage growth over time.

The CMMC Level 1, for instance, allows for self-attestation which means that you can begin your cybersecurity journey without paying for third-party auditors who crawl through your business to verify your compliance.

That carrot, however, comes with a big stick. By 2023, all businesses that participate directly or indirectly in the Department of Defense (DoD) supply chain must be compliant with the CMMC levels consistent with their access to Controlled Unclassified Information (CUI).

That will likely not be your business. Yet, having a security program based on the requirements that government contractors use is not a bad thing.

For this and other best practice reasons, CMMC Level 1 will be the standard to which I'll demonstrate compliance in this book.

The CMMC Level 1 Domains

An area of concern in a framework is called a *"domain."* Domains define an overall goal or focus for the practices recommended.

For the CMMC Level 1, we have the following domains:

- **Physical Protection (PE)**

  All security begins in the physical world. If someone has unfettered access to a device nothing can protect the contents. It is important to view your physical space as part of your cybersecurity solution. Take active steps to ensure that you know who, what, when, where, and how about your workspace when handling sensitive information.

- **Identification and Authentication (IA)**

  You must be able to identify who and what to build a robust response. Devices (laptops, phones, computers) and people must be identified with unique values (such as usernames). When there is an incident to be investigated, you want to recognize the actors involved.

- **Access Control (AC)**

  Protection begins with setting the rules. Modern operating systems and systems have security providers which allow or deny actions based on assigned rights. Logging on to a computer is allowed because you identify yourself as someone who has been given the right to log on. Understanding what controls and limits you can implement is the whole cybersecurity objective in a nutshell.

- **System And Communications Protection (SC)**

  The way you set up your information systems is important to cybersecurity. Every business has two zones: the public zone is where anonymous users interact with our business information, and the secure—or private—zone is where the business protects intellectual property, customer personally identifying information (PII), and trade secrets. These two zones must have strict rules for interacting with each other. That is where your cybersecurity plan comes into play.

- **System and Information Integrity (SI)**

  Vulnerabilities come in many forms. Unfortunately, we are not in control of what vulnerabilities exist and how they can be exploited. For that reason, we must always maintain our systems rather than believing that because we haven't been harmed in the past that we won't be in the future. New exploits of existing systems are discovered every day. We practice good maintenance to make sure we are ready.

- **Media Protection (MP)**

  The CMMC model covers the complete birth-to-death arc of protected information. The environment must maintain good protection throughout the whole lifespan of the data it is designed to protect. This includes the proper destruction of the media that housed the data. The fact that the media has gone beyond its useful life does not mean that the data it contained has.

COMPLIANCE 101

Most of us want to be independent, making our own decisions. Compliance feels like the opposite, an effort to take away our power.

We comply, not because it comes naturally to us but because we fear the consequences.

In cybersecurity, there is no room for rationalizing. It doesn't matter whether you believe your password is hard to crack or not. A computer in the hands of an attacker will determine whether that is true or not.

"Efficiency is doing things right;
EFFECTIVENESS *is doing the*
right things."
--Peter Drucker

When we follow compliance standards, we engage in risk management or risk transfer. We should view each practice as a commitment to reducing our risk.

As a business owner, you should recognize the importance of that. You are a business owner because you are willing to believe that risk can be managed. Now, you need to prove it.

Businesses risk failing every day. The fact that they don't is tied to the efforts the business stakeholders take to avoid doing risky things. We don't know what specific action or non-action leads to ultimate failure, so we are diligent at doing the right things.

Compliance is one way that we address this risk in the cyber world. It is a unique opportunity in the sense that by becoming compliant we can address all four ways of responding to risk: avoidance, acceptance, mitigation, and transference.

Consider the issue of Cybersecurity Insurance.

When you purchase a cyber insurance policy, you are transferring the costs of responding to a cyber incident from your resources to those of your insurer. The analysis finds that the average cost of a cyber incident to a business is more than $900,000.

Having an insurance policy for that is vital to most businesses. Of course, as the business scales, so do the costs of having a data breach. At all levels of business, you will need to consider the value of an insurance policy to protect your enterprise.

The insurance companies, however, have learned in the marketplace that writing cyber policies is not a simple source of revenue. Unlike natural disasters, the risks are harder to quantify because they are 100% human-caused.

To manage that risk, the insurers need to be persuaded that those who are paying for coverage are not engaged in risky behavior that would lead to a claim. That is when they turn to best practices. And that returns us to the frameworks like the Cyber Maturity Model.

Compliance becomes the demonstration that business stakeholders offer to the insurance provider. They are active participants in lowering the insurer's risk in return for having financial and procedural support should a security incident occur.

Three-Legged Stool

Creating a cybersecurity compliance program has been compared to a three-legged stool. Without all three of the legs, you do not have a stable stool.

Policy

Our first leg is **policy**. A policy is a written statement that defines a commitment to the goals of good cybersecurity practice.

The policy should be written to the specific needs and situation of the business for whom it is written. For example, while every person should practice creating strong passwords, every person's motivation and expression of why this is important will be unique.

The policy engages us at a personal or emotional level which is important for our follow-through. When the policy represents an organization, you are also creating a cultural bond that helps the team internalize good cyber hygiene.

Procedure

The second element of a cybersecurity plan is the **procedure**. These are the specific step-by-step instructions that we create to achieve the ideal that we write about in the policy.

Procedures should be clearly described, easily executed, and verifiable to ensure that they have been followed. In the lifetime of the cybersecurity plan, the procedures are the tasks that individual users internalize into their daily habits.

Evidence

The final leg of our stool is the most important for the protection of the business. It is not enough to say that you have a plan or that you do things that implement the plan. If you want insurance that will protect your interests, you must be able to provide undeniable proof that you did what you said you would do.

Evidence comes in the form of the configuration of computers to enforce policy, logs—both manual and digital—that provide time and place context for users and automated systems, and documented results from scans to show that vulnerabilities have been removed.

In a review of cybersecurity incidents and cyber insurance claims, 49% of the policies were not fully paid out because there was a lack of evidence that the cybersecurity policy had been followed.

Personal Protection Equipment (PPE)

Policy, **Procedure**, and **Evidence** are the PPE for your business. Your work is your life, and you must do everything you can to protect that. If you are not continually improving your cybersecurity, you are putting everything else at risk.

PART II

GUIDE TO PART II

In Part II, I'll provide a template for creating your first cybersecurity plan. Each chapter is a policy defined by the CMMC that you should have for your personal or business protection.

If you follow along, writing out answers to the questions and topics, you will be writing your policy document. It is important, though, that you let go of the fear of doing it wrong. In cybersecurity, fatalism--the belief that a cybersecurity incident is inevitable--is the enemy.

Any movement in the right direction is better than no action at all.

You will find in the following chapters that I have provided an outline to create momentum. If you take the time to think about the concepts, write responses to the questions, and gather the results into a clear statement of purpose and action, you will take a huge leap in ensuring that you will not be a statistic.

The Pattern

The following chapters will have this pattern:

Objective:= *I'll describe to you the context of the policy that you are building. This is how you will know what the boundaries are for your decisions.*

Priming The Pump:= *Next, I will ask a series of questions that can help you create the raw materials for your policy document. The more you spend on the detail in your answers, the easier it will be to write your coherent policy document.*

Outline the Policy:= *I'll provide you with a notated outline of what the policy structure should be to cover the subject matter.*

Discussion:= *Next, I'll provide background and suggest things that you should be aware of as you write your policy.*

Summarize:= *Finally, I'll wrap up the chapter with some final thoughts and a key take-a-way review of what you have been working on.*

Let's get started on our first plan...

PHYSICAL PROTECTIONS (PE)

Physical protections address the access your customers and employees have to your information systems.

PE Objectives

- Organize the physical space to provide appropriate barriers between people and information systems.
- Provide escorts when guests enter secured areas of your business.
- Record all entries and exits from secure areas with an appropriate logging system.
- Maintain records regarding the devices that give physical access to system resources—keys, locks, combinations, card readers, etc.

Priming the Pump

- Create a physical map of your work environment. Mark areas where sensitive information is processed. Locate barriers that can be utilized or constructed to separate systems from public areas.
- Document how guests are to be met, signed in,

badged, and escorted through secured areas of the business.

· Establish a logging process for entry and exit from secured areas. Define an appropriate log retention policy to ensure that physical access can be determined during a cybersecurity incident.

· Create a system for checking out and returning physical access devices to the physical environment. (Think keys to locks, access cards, etc.)

Policy Outline

1.1 Policy Purpose
Describe your goal for providing a secure physical environment.

1.2 Applies To: *What assets does this policy apply to?*

1.3 Physical Environment

1.3.1 Public Areas
Describe the areas of your business that are open to unescorted public patrons.

1.3.2 Private Areas
Describe the areas that are limited to business personnel or escorted visitors.

1.3.3 Secured System Areas
Describe the areas that require special permissions and authentication to access—even for the business personnel.

1.3.4 Cloud Security
Describe the means and access requirements for any cloud-based assets.

1.4 Monitoring Systems

1.4.1 <u>Video Monitors</u>
Describe all video-based monitors that you use to create a visual record of your environment.

1.4.2 <u>Alarm Systems</u>
Describe the boundary system that you use to control access during non-business hours.

1.4.3 <u>Other Services</u>
Describe all other services that you have applied that can assess when someone has been at the business location.

1.5 Physical Access Control

1.5.1 <u>Security Devices (keys, doors, etc.)</u>
Describe the devices that secure the boundaries of the physical business.

1.5.2 <u>Device Check-Out Procedures</u>
Describe the goals for issuing the devices that provide access to the physical business location to authorized personnel.

1.5.3 <u>Device Return Procedures</u>
Describe the goals for gathering all physical access devices when authorized personnel are separated from the business.

1.5.4 <u>Lost Device Procedures</u>
Describe what should occur and why when an access device has been irretrievably lost.

1.6 Guest Security Controls

1.6.1 <u>Sign In Procedures</u>
Create the justification for requiring guests who will be visiting secure areas of the business to provide appropriate information so their visit

can be traced.

1.6.2   Guest Badges
Establish the rule for requiring visible emblems to be worn by guests when they are on-premise and visiting secured areas.

1.6.3   Sign Out Procedures
Establish rules for guests to "log out" at the location where they signed in to confirm that they have left the premises of the business.

1.6.4   Guest Escort Procedures
Establish the rules around escorting all guests when they are in private or secured areas of the business.

1.7 Mobile Device Policy

1.7.1   Devices Covered Policy (phones, laptops, tablets)
Establish rules around the types of mobile devices that must be managed by the IT Services of the business—including whether personal devices of the personnel of the business can be used and are governed by the same control measures.

1.7.2   Physical Security Procedures
Establish the rules about how mobile devices are to be secured against unauthorized access by any not governed by the cybersecurity policies of the business.

1.7.3   Lost Device Procedures
Establish the rules around the event of a device becoming irretrievably lost to the business.

Discussion

Physical security is a challenging domain for many small businesses. Humans are wired to lead with trust when dealing with others. It can seem awkward to think about how we treat friends and strangers around our business when writing our cyber policies.

However, every small business has the potential to become a big business. As the business grows we do not know everyone at first sight. If you begin consideration of how to implement physical security when you are small, when you grow, you will only need to adjust the detail.

With physical security, the most important detail is how you create the evidence you can show that physical security practices have been followed. The good news is that many cost-friendly video security systems can help.

Validating who had physical control of your systems when a cybersecurity incident occured is the foundation of being able transfer the impact of recovery to a third party.

When writing out the policy, be sure to write some statement in response to all of the potential areas of concern. For instance, if you work out of your home, be sure to respond to the Guest Security Procedures even if you only state that you don't implement specific procedures. By stating that Guest Security practices are not required at this time, you state your policy and leave a reminder that such policies may change as your business situation changes.

Thoroughness is important.

Summary

Physical security is always important in your cybersecurity plan. When threat actors gain physical control of your systems, most security procedures become moot. The threat actor can dismantle protections at his or her leisure.

The physical security systems begin with the physical building where the systems reside. It's important to also recognize that you may have multiple security zones within the business. Some areas are public where very little control or monitoring can take place. Others are moderately secured, requiring some form of identification and logging before access. And some areas may be highly secured and include both logging and visual surveillance.

Defense in depth is an important factor in planning physical security.

IDENTIFICATION & AUTHENTICATION (IA)

I dentification and Authentication addresses the manner in which authorized and non-authorized users are identified and their identities confirmed by the users and information systems in your organization.

IA Objectives

- Establish the practice to create identities/accounts for human and digital agents that have access to the resources of the organization.
- Establish the practices and tools to ensure that the identities used for access to resources are the real users and not a threat actors with compromised credentials.

Priming The Pump

- How do you distinguish between human users and computerized agents with usernames?
- What is your current list of users for both groups?
- Can you group your users into role-based

functions?
- What is the security mode in your environment-- workgroup or domain?
  - *Workgroup: individual computers that do not share any security information*
  - *Domain: individual computers are members of a security provider hosted on a server called a domain controller. Users can be created on the server and used on all member workstations in the domain.*
- What pattern will you use to ensure that all users have a unique name identifier over the life of the organization?
  - RobR could be Robert Ruder or Rob Renshaw. How do you deconflict the username? Example: RobR and RobR2 or Rob.Ruder and Rob.Renshaw, etc.
- What authentication methods will your organization use and why?
  - Passwords
  - Multi-Factor Authentication
  - Biometrics
- What practices will you follow to ensure that passwords—where appropriate—are sufficiently complex and changed frequently enough to protect the organization?
- Will you support password or authentication managers such as LastPass, etc?

Policy Outline

1.1 **Policy Purpose:** Describe the business case for this Cybersecurity Domain
The identification and Authorization policy is the

foundation of controlling the actors—digital and human—in the systems. This statement should establish the philosophy of why accounts and authentication methods must be supported by the organization.

1.2 Applies To: What assets (who) does this policy apply to?

1.3 User Accounts Policy

1.3.1 Required User Account Policy

Create a mandate that every asset has a user account in the system.

1.3.2 User Account Naming Conventions

Create a username pattern that scales as the business grows by not duplicating usernames.

1.3.3 Shared Account Policy

Address the need or practice of using the same account on different systems for different purposes or actors (generally this should not be common practice).

1.4 Account Creation Locations (where are they created?)

1.4.1 Account Locations

Describe where user accounts are created (workgroups are done on each device, domains can be done on the controller and shared by devices)

1.4.2 Account Groups

Describe a rationale for combining multiple accounts into groups that can be used by administrators to audit and assign user rights or activities on the devices.

1.4.3 User Account Lifecycle

1.4.3.1 Account Creation
Describe the timing and requirements for creating accounts.

1.4.3.2 Account Suspension
Describe the conditions that require an account to be suspended.

1.4.3.3 Account Deletion
Describe the conditions and purposes for deleting accounts.

1.4.4 Anonymous user account management
Describe circumstances when an anonymous user account may be used and the policies surrounding the care and maintenance of the same.

1.5 Authentication Methods

1.5.1 Passwords

1.5.1.1 Password General Practice
Describe the general principles of having strong passwords and the importance of good password protection practices to avoid exposing the business to threat actors.

1.5.1.2 Length requirement
Define the minimum password length

1.5.1.3 Complexity requirement
Define the password complexity requirements (capitals, numbers, non-alphanumerics, etc)

1.5.1.4 Change requirements
Define the password change parameters such as maximum and minimum ages, no

duplication requirements, etc.

1.5.1.5 Management practices

Describe the important management practices surrounding the care of passwords —don't write them down, don't share them, hide from others when entering them, etc.

1.5.2 Multi-factor Authentication

1.5.2.1 MFA Requirements

Describe the business case for using multi-factor authentication to increase the protection of critical accounts.

1.5.2.2 MFA Authorized Devices

Define what devices can be used as the alternative factor for authentication.

1.5.2.3 MFA Security Requirements

Define the accounts that must be protected using MFA.

1.5.2.4 MFA Recovery Requirements

Create the requirements for creating recovery procedures for all MFA-protected accounts so that lost or broken devices do not create a crisis for the business.

1.5.3 Biometrics

1.5.3.1 Biometric Requirements

Describe the business case for the use of biometrics to connect a person physically to their account.

1.5.3.2 Biometric Authorized Devices

Define what biometrics are supported and what devices will be used to confirm identities.

1.5.3.3 Biometric Recovery Practices

Describe the business case for having recovery procedures to restore access to devices or accounts if the person identified is no longer able to access the system.

Discussion

The Identification and Authorization policy is the foundation of the whole cybersecurity plan. If we do not know who and we can't confirm that they are who they say they are, how can we begin to say whether they are authorized or not? Every security plan begins with the actors in the system.

You should know specifically at this moment, and generally, for the life of your enterprise, who it is that has access to your systems. While something as basic as Usernames and Passwords is not the ideal security method, they remain the most universal way to start every security plan.

Modern methods have now expanded to include physical traits, aka biometrics such as fingerprints, eye patterns, etc. Those methods must still connect us to an account that is used to assign the rights or permissions. So, you should address what biometrics are allowed and how the associated accounts can be recovered should the biometric data become lost.

Multifactor authentication is also a popular way to reinforce the value of having user accounts by creating a physical device for the user identified. If this is an option (or a requirement) for your organization, you should establish not only what methods are supported but also who owns and manages the devices that are allowed as the additional authentication factors.

The result of your IA policy should provide any auditor the ability to evaluate whether systems can be accessed by unauthorized users. Watch for things like anonymous user accounts, shared credentials, or other conveniences which circumvent the intended protections.

Summary

Identification and Authentication are the beginning of all security planning. If we do not know who, how can we know what and when?

Your policy should provide flexibility for change. The technology for logging on to a system is always ripe for re-invention.

It is also important that your policy address the question of external information systems. You will not always have control to enforce identity and authentication practices, but you should expand your policy to cover those situations. Retail, bank, and productivity software that is provided as online services can expose your internal systems if users do not vary their passwords between online and local systems.

Start with a strong IA policy and your cybersecurity plan will be resilient.

ACCESS CONTROL (AC)

A ccess control determines how you organize your business to provide the appropriate confidentiality required by the information assets you manage in your organization.

AC Objectives

- Limit access to your security systems to authorized users.
- Restrict users' transactions and functions consistent with their job description.
- Define the applications and information systems users are authorized to use.
- Establish a public information policy to control the publication of business data.

Priming The Pump

- What roles or groups define the organization of your business and business info?
- How do you organize the information you manage daily: Department, Revenue, Source, other?
- What type of transactional access do your roles or groups need in each category of information: No

Access, Read, Write, Modify, Delete?
- What applications do each of your roles or groups need and why?
- What are the authorized uses for each application?
- Map applications to the jobs/roles in your organization.
- Describe the ways that external (owned by others) applications can be managed for security practices.
- What information can be published to a public access location like a web server?
- What information should be restricted from publication to a web server?
- What procedures can be followed to determine whether information falls under the publish or no-publish restrictions?
- What roles or groups are authorized to publish information?

Policy Outline

1.1 **Policy Purpose:** Describe the business purpose of this policy

   In general terms, the Access Control policy describes who, what, when, and where. These are discretionary policies that describe the access that individual users or groups have to the business assets such as devices, documents, proprietary knowledge, etc.

1.2 **Applies To**: Who does this policy apply to?

1.3 **System Policy**

   1.3.1   <u>Authorized User</u>

Create your declaration that the systems and devices of the organization are only for the intended business purposes and by the AUTHORIZED users.

1.3.1.1 System Access Rights
Establish a process for how system access rights are determined and the circumstances when they can be revoked.

1.3.2 Secure System Notifications
Create a policy that all digital systems must contain appropriate notification that they are only for the use of authorized persons or systems.

1.4 Authorized Applications

1.4.1 Authorized Applications List
Create the authority to control the applications that are to be used and supported for the benefit of the organization.

1.4.1.1 Internal Systems
Establish authority for determining which applications can be installed on systems owned by the organization.

1.4.1.2 External Systems
Establish an authority for determining which applications and systems that are not governed by the organization may be accessed.

1.4.2 Shared Resources (SR) Policy
Create the authority for reviewing and determining when it is appropriate for multiple users or systems to share assets.

1.4.2.1 SR Categories Policy

Establish the principles for groups of related assets that may be shared by multiple users or groups in the organization.

1.4.2.2 SR Permissions Policy

Establish the principles for how shared assets will be managed for permissions and rights in keeping with the other requirements of the cybersecurity policies of the organization.

1.4.3 File Encryption Policy

Create the authority to establish practices and procedures to encrypt sensitive data while in motion and at rest within the systems controlled by the organization. This should include the need for technologies such as SSL and drive encryption.

1.5 External Systems Policy

1.5.1 External Use Policy

Establish the authority and rationale for limiting the use of systems that are not under the direct control of the organization.

1.5.1.1 Allowed Uses

Establish a review process for creating a maintaining a list of allowed uses for external systems in the normal procedures of the organization.

1.5.1.2 Restricted Uses and Conditions

Establish a similar review process for establishing procedures to restrict access to external systems that are not supported by the organization.

1.5.2   Personal Use Device Policy (BYOD)
Establish the organizational authority to define the purposes and use of devices that are owned by the personnel in the organization. Most importantly, establish the justification for private devices to be brought under management by the organization to protect digital assets.

   1.5.2.1 Authorized Devices
   Create a process for identifying private devices which may be used under the policy to access organizational assets.

   1.5.2.2 Allowed Uses
   Create the justifications for what uses BYOD devices can be used for and how they are to be monitored and maintained.

   1.5.2.3 Prohibited Uses
   Establish the principles for what types of uses are not allowed by the organization on privately owned devices.

1.6 Public Information Publishing Policy

   1.6.1   Sensitive Information Management Restrictions
   Establish the principles and governance of information publishing to publicly accessible systems such as websites and social media.

   1.6.2   Public Data Posting Decision Procedure
   Create the decision control mechanisms for making decisions about what information can be published to the public.

   1.6.3   Authorized Public Information Posting
   Create a governing committee that can provide

authorization for information to be published.

Discussion

Access Control is about software and data. Software controls what we can do with a system.

Operating Systems include security services that enforce what users can and cannot do. Permissions such as the right to log on, the right to remote access, or the right to change settings are just some of the options you have as a system administrator.

Additionally, you can control access by pre-determining what software is installed. Users cannot violate the cybersecurity plan if the software means to do so is not present. Each piece of software represents unknown risks and vulnerabilities. By limiting what is installed, you reduce your risks substantially.

At the data leve, transactions users perform are represented by the following:

No-Access: The system denies access if no combination of user identity and group membership does not grant access to the resource.

Access Denied: Active response when a DENY permission has been specified for a user identity or group. Any DENY permission overrides all GRANTs.

Read: The ability to view the content of the resource is allowed.

Write: The ability to create new content.

Update: The ability to change the contents of a resource.

Delete: The ability to remove a resource from the

system.

Additional consideration should be given to the use of encryption to protect PII data. Industry practice says that data should be encrypted while in motion and at rest. Without encryption, physical control of the resources, such as hard drives or email attachments represents the potential for a cybersecurity incident. A robust encryption policy can save you serious amounts of damage to your reputation and organizational survival.

Finally, you should always have a specific procedure for vetting information that is shared on public forums such as your website or social media accounts. History has recorded that some of the largest cybersecurity data breaches occurred because what should have been private information was transferred—intended to be temporary— to a public server. A clear separation plan that carefully controls the plan and execution of posting information to public resources is important.

Summary

Your Access Control (AC) policy focuses on 4 key features:

1. System behavior enforced by the Operating System –Local Security
2. Authorized Applications and Data Permissions
3. External systems (applications and hardware not controlled by the business)
4. Public Data Publishing –website, social media, etc.

It is important to break your business down into logical workflows so that you can identify which users/accounts require the specific permissions to be successful.

Even if your users wear multiple hats in the organization, you should not build the policy for what they do today but for the scale of the organization in the future. It's always easier to be overly specific today and grow into it.

SYSTEMS & COMMUNICATION PROTECTION (SC)

Systems and Communications protections create boundaries between the electronic users and services that are necessary to conduct business.

SC Objectives

- Create monitoring, control, and protection at the organizational boundaries as appropriate for the information that is being maintained.
- Isolate internal resources that require public access (email, website, etc.) from the rest of the secured network resources.

Priming The Pump

- Where does your organization connect to the Internet?
- Does the device that connects you to the Internet monitor and restricts the traffic that flows from the Internet inward towards your internal

systems?

- Do your workstations have an active firewall running?
- How often do you review reports or logs to determine if someone has been trying to access your system from the outside world?
- Does your organization host public content within the physical network where private or secured data is also managed?
- Create a list of services or resources that should be publicly available to anonymous users.
- Do you create a separate network of public services from the protected ones?

Policy Outline

1.1 **Policy Purpose:** *Create the business justification to control the flow of information into and out of the organization's network(s).*

1.2 **Applies To:** *Who does this policy apply to?*

1.3 **Firewall Policy:**
Establish the organizational need to protect internal systems from threat actors.

    1.3.1   Required Firewall Policy:
    Create the requirement that all networks and devices are protected from external access based on industry best practices.

    1.3.2   Firewall Monitoring Requirement:
    Describe how the firewall will be monitored for intrusion attempts and unauthorized data transfers.

1.4 Subnet Policy:

Establish the governance principles that protected systems accessed by external users (email, website, etc) must be logically separated on the network from solely private systems—also known as a Demilitarized Zone (DMZ).

1.4.1 DMZ Policy:

Define which systems should be within a DMZ

1.4.2 DMZ Public Access:

Define what public access should be granted

1.4.3 DMZ Protected Access:

Describe conditions that allow protected systems into the DMZ

Discussion

Firewalls are extremely important to your cybersecurity plan. The network protocols that created the Internet were designed at a time when the way things connected was more important than the concern for the way that the connections would be used.

The Internet is based on eternal optimism. The most important threat at the time it was created was the loss of connection from one point to another. Unfortunately, the times have changed. Those who use their skills for harm are just as active as those who seek good.

It is important, therefore, that we lock down our systems, ensuring that our risks are limited to areas where we must accept some risk or that we have done the best we can to mitigate vulnerabilities.

A firewall is one such way to 'lock down' a network environment or device. Requests that we initiate are sent out to the Internet and returned to us so that we can view websites, send an email, and run web-based productivity applications. But those who would troll our systems trying to find weaknesses are blocked by the protective bubble that we create with our firewall.

Firewalls can also be layered to add additional protection. While a firewall at the Internet connection protects all the systems within a network, a firewall implemented on a laptop protects that device even if it is used somewhere other than the business network. This is important for those who travel with their devices and use publicly hosted Internet services like "free wifi."

A robust firewall policy addresses all devices and requires an active firewall at all times that the device is in use.

Summary

The Systems and Communications policy is about firewalls. Know where yours are and make sure that they are turned on to protect you from bad actors.

Two particular firewalls are important:

- The organizational firewall that sits between you and the Internet when you are working within the protected network.
- The local device firewall protects you when you are away from the control of the organization, and you use Internet resources that belong to other organizations.

SYSTEM & INFORMATION INTEGRITY (SI)

System and Information Integrity addresses the mechanisms required to maintain a high confidence that the information and systems are consistent with the intentional change necessary and not as a result of an attack by an unauthorized agent.

SI Objectives

- Maintain your systems by running regular software updates to eliminate known vulnerabilities.
- Install a malware protection system that can scan your system for known malware or detect and respond to unexpected activity that might be an indication of a malware attack.
- Establish a routine of updating the malware protection system to ensure that it has the latest signatures and logic to detect new threats.
- Create routine scans that include a deep inspection of all the files on your system to determine if malware has been downloaded

or installed on your system without your knowledge.

Priming The Pump

- What antivirus/antimalware do you currently run?
- Is your AV licensed so that it can download current signatures and perform scans on your system?
- What do you know about the difference between Antivirus/Antimalware and Endpoint Detection and Response (EDR)? Google it.
- When does your current AV/EDR run a system scan for hidden malware?
- How do you collect logs from your scans to show an auditor that you are actively seeking to detect and respond to malware?
-

Policy Outline

1.1   Policy Purpose:
Create the organizational requirement that the integrity of the organization's system is always maintained.

1.2   Applies To: Who or what does this policy apply to?

1.3   **Patch Management:**
Establish the authority and mandate to keep all hardware and software updated with the most recent patches.

1.3.1 Patch Scan Policy:
Establish the principles of how frequently scans should be conducted to determine new software requirements.

1.3.2 Patch Application Policy:
Define the length of time between when an update is released and when it should be applied to all affected systems in the organization.

1.4 Antimalware Management:
Establish the principles for the organization to manage and maintain software to detect and respond to malicious code which may come into the organization. Create the necessary governance to require such software in all appropriate systems.

1.4.1 Antimalware Policy:
Describe which devices must have antimalware protection and who is authorized to decide on what protection is appropriate.

1.5 Antimalware Maintenance:
Establish the requirements for all antimalware to be maintained appropriately and promptly.

1.6 System Scanning Policy:
Describe the procedures for scheduled scans of files and the real-time scanning of downloads to ensure that they are free of malware. Also, create an authority to utilize alternate technologies that substantially create the same protection as that of antimalware.

1.6.1 Malicious Code Scanning Frequency:
Define the acceptable amount of time between

scheduled scans of network resources.

1.6.2 <u>Real-Time Scans:</u>
Describe how the antimalware product protects systems from malware when downloading, opening, or executing files.

Discussion

The SI policy addresses the **patch management** and **antimalware** practices that you use to address vulnerabilities in your systems. All software has the potential for a vulnerability that can lead to serious exploitation.

You cannot buy a system, deploy it, and then ignore it. It would be like buying a car and then never performing any maintenance at all on it. For quite a while that may seem doable, but eventually, the oil, tires, engine, cooling, etc. will break, and then your costs will be much larger than if you perform routine maintenance.

The key to this domain is to understand what software you have chosen to provide the patches and the anti-virus protections. Once you have that determined, then you need to follow the best practices offered by the vendors to ensure that your systems are being maintained.

Your answers to these questions will be reviewed for appropriateness and should reflect at least a monthly attention to the questions regarding active protections. The better news is that most Patch and AV management offer automated scheduling for the various scans and fixes that they provide.

Summary

Maintenance of your systems is the critical focus of this cybersecurity domain. It's easy to believe that you are being protected when you are not. But it is also easy to set up services that will perform these updates for you so that you will know that you are being protected.

The key will be automating the process to ensure that you are OK.

MEDIA PROTECTION (MP)

Media protections address the complete lifecycle (birth to death) of information and information systems within the organization.

MP Objectives

- Provide a decommissioning or destruction procedure that ensures all digital information is rendered unusable at the end of life for all digital systems and resources.

Priming The Pump

- How many hard drives, USB thumb drives, or DVD/CDROM media do you possess that have business data on them?
- Does your town or city have businesses that provide paper document storage and shredding services? Which ones are they?
- Do you work in an industry where there are very strict confidentiality or document management requirements? What information do you have on the destruction requirements?

Policy Outline

1.1 **Policy Purpose:**
Establish the governance principle that data must be protected through its life cycle. This includes its destruction beyond any use.

1.2 **Applies To:** *Who does this policy apply to in the organization?*

1.3 **Media Destruction Policy:**
Describe the business requirements for destroying media at the end of its productive life.

    1.3.1 **Removable Media Destruction:**
    Describe the destruction requirements for media such as USB drives and CDROM/DVDs.

    1.3.2 **HD/SSD Drive Destruction:**
    Describe the detail and requirements for destroying fixed drive devices.

    1.3.3 **Destruction Certification:**
    Describe your certification requirements when using a 3-party to handle the destruction of media.

Discussion

Study after study has demonstrated that many attempts to simply delete data when it is no longer needed is not an effective way to keep the files out of the hands of bad actors. The only proof positive way to eliminate the risk is to physically destroy the media in a manner that it cannot be used ever again.

Cutting, chipping, breaking open and shredding are the

mechanisms that you should consider in your policy.

Summary

Cybersecurity is a birth-to-death process and understanding how the media is destroyed is an important piece of your plan.

PART III

CYBERSECURITY POLICY TEMPLATE

*The following is a sample cybersecurity policy for the **CMM Media Protection** domain. I offer it as a model for building your cybersecurity policies. Policies should always reflect your own business goals, motivations, and resources because you are putting your reputation on the line, and doing what comes naturally to you is better than writing words that you don't practice.*

[ORGANIZATION] MEDIA PROTECTION POLICY

1.1 Purpose: [Organization] gathers and creates sensitive customer and business information while conducting normal business activities. This information has a productive life and then it should be destroyed completely to protect the stakeholders of that information. This policy describes the principles for the effective destruction of ALL MEDIA that may or may not contain personally identifiable information or sensitive business information.

Combined with the appropriate media destruction procedures, this policy will be the authorized manner for handling all storage media.

1.2 Applies To: This policy applies to ALL members of [Organization]. Failure to comply with this policy may be used as grounds for dismissal from [Organization]. Egregious abuse of the information covered by this policy may also be referred to the appropriate civil authorities for prosecution under the laws of the United States and the relevant local jurisdiction.

1.3 Policy: This organization intends to put all PII and sensitive corporate information beyond the reach of anyone at the end of its useful life. All forms of storage both paper and digital must be rendered unreadable by any means. The following principles are established to ensure that goal.

1.3.1 Paper documents: Paper documents that have exceeded their retention periods should be shredded using a "confetti" method which eliminates the ability to restore them to a readable format. This destruction may be done in-house or with an appropriate vendor who provides certified destruction of documents.

1.3.2 HD/SSD Drive Destruction: Magnetic Drives (HDDs) and Solid-State Drives (SSDs) must be degaussed and/or shredded at the end of their retention period. It is not the policy of the [Organization] organization to use digital erasure to wipe the content of the drives and repurpose them. A third party may be used to provide the destruction of these drives if they have a certified procedure for handling sensitive information.

1.3.3 Removable Media Destruction: Removable media such as USB drives, CD-ROMs, or DVDs must be destroyed beyond functional use. Destruction may be done in-house following accepted procedures or may be conducted by a certified third party.

1.3.4 Destruction Certificates: When an authorized third party is used to destroy physical media, it is appropriate to request and pay for a *Certificate of Destruction* to retain for liability purposes. Certificates should be retained for a length of time not less than the original retention period of the data that was destroyed.

The policy document above is offered as a model in tone and content for any policy document that you create to protect your business.

Again, I will emphasize that slavishly copying a sample document does not protect your business because mitigating or transferring your risk requires that you do what you say.

Policy documents must be combined with documented procedures for executing the policy. And then there should be appropriate documentation of the procedures being followed in the form of evidence that can be shown to any authority who requests it.

In the following chapter, I'll describe how you can improve your business security by conducting an audit of your policies and procedures before an incident occurs.

A CYBERSECURITY AUDIT GUIDE

I n the chapter Compliance 101, I made a case to call compliance a three-legged stool where Policy, Practice, and Evidence come together to demonstrate your competence in practicing good cyber hygiene.

Compliance with Level 1 of the CMMC is generally planned to be a self-attestation. That is those of us who are practicing the principles of Level 1 simply make a public statement that we have implemented all the practices.

However, this requirement of self-attestation is only a means to encourage all businesses to adopt the practices with as little fuss as necessary. It is certainly challenging to go through an external audit.

I have worked with clients who have spent 12-18 months working on implementing the practices of the ISO 27001 Cybersecurity standard.

Demonstrating compliance with an audit, however, is the best way to prove to your customers and your vendors that you are taking cybersecurity seriously.

This chapter will be an overview of the goals and procedures of having an independent auditor inspect your policy and organization for compliance with the CMMC Level 1 standard. It is a good practice for you to run this process as a desktop exercise within your business.

Assessment Procedures

Assessing cybersecurity practices involves three elements: *the assessment objective, the methods established to comply* with the objective, and *objects that can be collected* to confirm the methods. In other words: policy, practice, and evidence. An auditor uses these elements, combined with industry best practices, to decide whether the documented practice meets the objective of the standard.

It is important to note that compliance is not a straitjacket. There are many ways to comply with the objectives that can be unique to your organization. Don't sweat the details. Find a fiscally responsible way to meet the intent of the objective; and actively demonstrate that you are doing it.

An auditor will generally take the standard that you are seeking certification for and go through the practices one by one to determine the level of your compliance.

An auditor will begin by asking to see specific artifacts (documents, people, configuration files, etc) that establish your commitment to the standard.

Assessment Objects (expected to be presented on request)

- **Specifications:** Your documents-based evidence of compliance which includes policies, procedures, security plans, security requirements, functional specifications, and architectural designs associated with the objective.

- **Mechanisms:** The hardware, software, or firmware safeguards that are employed within the system.
- **Activities:** the protection-related actions that support the security of the system that are carried out by the people.
- **People:** The individuals or groups of individuals who are tasked with applying the specifications, mechanisms, or activities to meet the assessment objective.

Next, the auditor will use assessment to determine the level of awareness, application, and effectiveness of the security plan provided.

Assessment Methods (actions the auditor will take)

- **Examine:** the auditor will review the documents to assess whether they represent a reasonable response to the security objectives.
- **Interview:** the auditor will hold discussions with the people identified in the policies to determine if they clearly understand the requirements assigned to them and how to effectively complete them.
- **Test:** The auditor will ask to see the security mechanisms in action to determine that they are fully functional. This may include having personnel demonstrate the activities they are to carry out or quiz them on specific procedures.

The auditor will be responsible for determining the depth of the examination. He/she will determine what is appropriate among the following levels:

- **Basic:** This is a review of the high-level

application of cybersecurity practices. Documents are evaluated on their application to generally accepted security requirements, activities, and knowledge. The goal is to ensure that practices are free from obvious errors and that individuals are committed to conducting business in a security-conscious way.

- **Focused:** The examination begins with the basic analysis outlined above but then involves a more in-depth study and analysis of the mechanisms and functional-level implementation. The goal of this analysis is to provide grounds for an increased level of confidence that the security plan provided will achieve the protections that are promised and implemented correctly to do so.
- **Comprehensive:** This examination goes beyond the objectives outlined in the Focused review to include a detailed and thorough examination of the implementation. Extensive documentation will be requested to assess whether the security plan will deliver the safeguards promised. The goals of a comprehensive audit will be that the practices are not only correctly implemented and free from obvious defects, but also that they are being followed consistently as the foundation of a continuous improvement project to increase the effectiveness of the safeguards.

The assessment process generates a lot of stress. Importantly, remember that stress is your response to the outcome you want to achieve. No one likes to put their future into the hands of another individual. It is not natural.

However, the way to reduce the stress is to invest more in the process that leads up to the assessment. Become a cybersecurity student. Study the standard and find a variety of examples of how other organizations have met the standard.

Educate your stakeholders. Don't implement written procedures and security software without providing training to your personnel who are expected to implement them daily.

Remember, your purpose for implementing a cybersecurity plan is to demonstrate to others that you are a low-risk organization. Whether that assessment is an insurance company providing a cyber insurance policy or a prospect who is risking their privacy to do business with you, you want to be able to show them that you are a trustworthy person with whom to do business.

CONCLUSION

I t's time to go back to the beginning.

Why did you pick up this book?

If I put myself in your shoes, I know that there is an important step I want to take in my business. I want to expand. I need to take on a larger client. Or I need to protect my personal and business interests by purchasing a cyber insurance policy.

All of these are important reasons to transfer my risk and take the time to create a cybersecurity plan.

What I want to say to you now is that it's ok to feel overwhelmed. You don't have to be a computer expert to have a security plan. You don't have to be an expert of anything.

Sure, you will have work to do. And you will read a lot of technical words that don't appear to be useful to your line of business. I want to encourage you, however, to be patient with the process.

You can find a mentor. There are managed services providers who can work with you to answer the questions and complete the implementation of a good cybersecurity plan.

Only you, however, can provide the force of will. Whether

you are self-employed or the head of a modest but growing concern, it is important that you be committed to a continuous improvement process.

Business and management consultant Eliyahu Goldratt advocated that every business should be based on this continuous improvement vision. He referred to the resistance you feel when implementing change as a bottleneck. But every business should view itself as part of a continuous flow.

As a manager of that flow, the most important task is identifying THE bottleneck that limits the current flow and then eliminating it.

At this point, you most likely are the bottleneck in your cybersecurity.

Challenge the assumptions change is not possible or that you are not a target. The risks you face are not some news headline. They are potential events that could end your business.

Your business success will ultimately rest on your ability to embrace and implement plans that address the confidentiality, integrity, and availability of your information systems.

So, today, make the decision to follow the guidelines in this book and make the changes you need to implement a cybersecurity plan. Then, start.

Write your steps out in a list. Do the first thing. Then scratch it off the list.

And if you need some help, find a professional. Or, follow the links in the Resources section to continue your study with online course materials that I've prepared to get you through your cybersecurity policy process.

ABOUT THE AUTHOR

Robert Ruder

Robert Ruder has 30+ years of experience in the information systems industry as an author, trainer, architect, developer, and business consultant.

Robert is an adjunct faculty member of the Gonzaga University School of Business Administration. He also holds several industry certifications including the Certified in Cybersecurity by the (ISC)2 organization, an international organization devoted to promoting professional IT/IS ethics and improving cybersecurity in all businesses.

His business, IDIC Designs, LLC is devoted to helping small business owners master the Infiinte Diversity and Infintite Combinations of technology solutions that make small businesses thrive and profit in the marketplace.

RESOURCES

I have prepared several online resources to help the readers of this book to write their first cybersecurity policies. These resources are free to all who want to join a growing community of business owners devoted to continuous improvement of their online presence.

The following list is what you will find in the IDIC Designs Cybersecurity Toolbox.

- Cybersecurity Self-Assessment
- 5 Component Framework Asset Inventory Worksheets
- Self-paced Cybersecurity Policy eCourse
- Small Business Resilience Newletter

URL: https://bit.ly/cybersecurity-planning-book

On the following page you will find a QR code to access the resources.

QR Code for downloading your cybersecurity planning resources: